Survival

A New Beginning

Life After A stroke

One Person Person's journey:

 Chronicled through poetry.

By

John A. Yurgens

Introduction

 Many people have experienced their own personal storms to weather at some point in time. Many of us have "survived" any countless number of life altering events.

We all need love and support; I believe all human beings need to look out for each other; that's my calling is to offer support, kindness and encouragement to every Survivor I encounter.

Each Survivor has their own unique survival and Recovery story, including all the challenges that come with the "New Normal"

My survival came about from an intracranial hemorrhagic Stroke (an aneurism/ Brain bleed) resulting in cognitive, visual and physical impairments

As a means of coping with my survival and new normal. I began to write poetry about my journey. Since mine is a story of stroke survival, that was the initial impetus of my writings.

It took a while but I recognized other survivors (whatever the cause) might relate to some of my writing.

. Feel free to think of your own survival, while reading my poems. Please enjoy this insight into one person's survival journey perchance some may assist you, on your journey. Feel free to cOntact me, you can share your story with a

survivor that "understands" Contact information: E-mail:
jay4770@gmail.com

Acknowledgment

I need to thank my family: my wife, kay Anne, my four (4)
children, five (5) Grandchildren, and my extended family.
Your love and support has been amazing. My friends old and
new. Those who assisted with editing.   Thank you.

RK for helping me find my way out of my darkness.

The many survivors I have encountered through my
volunteer work and Support groups. I can only hope I
impacted your lives as profoundly as you impacted mine.

This is as it should be, as human beings, we are all in this together we need to look out for each other.

Several of these poems have been published already.

Several of my poems were originally published in Stroke Net; a monthly online newsletter for the stroke network. (Strokenetwork.org), Stroke misconnection a quarterly on-line magazine, American stroke association/ American Heart Association. Blue water Healthy Living a weekly online magazine. Port Huron, MI (bluewaterhealthyliving.org) is publishing many of my poems. All are printed here with permission.

DEDICATED

To

Kay Anne AND LA Familia

Body of book

Not alone

You are not alone

After being told you had a stroke

It s scary, uncertainty abounds, what's next?

Some may believe we are the only ones to ever experienced

this

What we are slogging through, nobody could ever

understand

Arrogance or ignorance? Perhaps a little of both.

We may think "I'm a strong person I can get through this!"

Although personal strength is not in question, it may prove

helpful along your journey;

All need to understand the mental, emotional and physical challenges are very real.

Once you realize there are other stroke survivors, a bond can develop almost immediately, upon meeting

We are all different, each with our individual life experiences

Every stroke, rehab and Recovery is different

We face challenges, without definitions others can understand. Hang onto connections mad with Fellow survivors, they understand.

We had a stroke! The life we Knew no longer exists

We must all recognize we are not alone.   Supporting each other anyway we can.

Loses

Grieving is an individual process, grieve at your own pace.

Only you know what you need, grieve your loses; fret not,

you are not alone. Many have been challenged with losses.

No need for side by side comparisons, we are all unique.

Much like grieving; everyone measures lose in their own

unique way. Do not dwell on all you have lost, focus your

energy on the positive, those things you love and still have

nthe ability to do.

Thoughts, feelings, fears and concerns shared with family

and friends; will help you through the challenges of today

and tomorrow, just as yesterday.

There are many reasons for loss and recovery. None funny;

but humorous situations arise; we need to learn to laugh at

them, without laughter there would surely be tears. The day may come when you feel free and comfortable enough to laugh at your own loses.

The emotional pain you feel right now, Will pass someday. Rest assured as the sun dawns days anew recognize your blessings, you are here to witness them. Take full advantage of your second chance at life. Make a difference every day. With a positive attitude and continued hard work and determination (okay stubbornness), there will be the potential to improve, along your journey. It will not be easy nor fast, but when those improvements come, as small as they may seem to others, they should be celebrated, like leaving THAT wheelchair behind, that first time and walking once again (even with assistance) Your journey may have bumps and unexpected road blocks. Trust your instincts. Accept support and encouragement of others. Some, perhaps wiser, may have traveled a similar path, they may

become that friend with whom you share your joys,

frustrations or concerns. Loses hurt but they don't need to

be crippling.

Memories

Some may be forgotten, others completely unknown still

more lost in the file room of the brain.

 good, bad, happy, sad, some better left unknown

Others come from family stories

 painful, joyful, Saddening, maddening, frightening

, They may Cause a: Smile, Frown, Laughter or even tears; do

not forsake them; embrace them.

Memories are the record of what brought you to here and

now.

We need to learn to live with and accept your memories.

Many will dissipate with time.

Beware of triggers; they ambush you. They may come from

sight or smell, specific events, a special song, or even simple

words. Be easy on yourself when these triggers disrupt your

day

With help and concentrated efforts those triggers may also

dissipate with time.

Now I See

Now I see

At least I try

Why my friends

Who saw me at my worst

Are so amazed to see me now

Many prepared for a world without me.

Of course they hoped and prayed

Yet they prepared just the same.

Alas here I am amongst the living

My work here not yet done!

HOPE

Everyone needs hope

Without hope we are left with only despair

Hope is not denial

Hope is the courage to continue….

Many learn to "live with" or even "accept" the here and now,

Still holding onto Hope.

Hope is beautiful and life sustaining.

Providing the conviction to persevere.

Journey

Every Journey begins with a single step

our journey is long, at times tedious other times fun.

Of course there may be Bumps, Pot holes, Roadblocks,

detours

Peaks and valleys, We have all overcome these obstacles,

 perhaps not all, but many just the same

There are times we may stumble along the way,

With or without assistance we need to get back up

 Brush off the dust and take another step

When discouragement and challenges attempt to overwhelm

us.

We need only look back at the obstacles we have overcome

to get to here and now

Celebrating all our victories, no matter how small.

We must remain focused on our purpose. With focused

purpose

Continued steps of progress are indeed possible

Simply put one foot in front of the other

Most often our steps are forward

Other times we may take few steps back

With hope, encouragement and

Support of others

We can continue progressing on our journey

One step at a time

Don't give up

Don't Give up!

 that's the easy way out

nothing ventured nothing gained

Nobody ever said recovery is easy

 recovery is not for sissies

it can be exhausting and exhilarating at the same time

okay at least within the same day or week

 We must never give up on ourselves

God did not give up on us

How can we justify doing so?

No goals

Without a goal

We find ourselves, Drifting like a song without a singer,

a soul without a mate

Without goals we are left

Aimlessly surviving?

Day in and day out

No goal to strive toward

No reason to get up and push forward.

So much easier said than done,

God is great, He will help us along our journey

But that journey and assistance will be of no use

If we fail to set our goals (hourly/daily/weekly etc.)

With those goals come mini victories

That help to push us on.

Darkness to light

It's Always darkest just before the dawn

A few years ago my life was darker than I ever recall

Then dawn came and the light of day was so sweet

We must survive the darkness to appreciate the light.

I give thanks daily for the gift of life I have been given

I can only hope and pray I can do justice to the gift of life.

This second chance I have been given.

Darkness to light

It's Always darkest just before the dawn

A few years ago, my life was darker than I ever recall

Then dawn came, and the light of day was so sweet

We must survive the darkness to appreciate the light.

I give thanks daily for the gift of life I have been given

I can only hope and pray I can do justice to the gift of life.

This second chance I have been given.

A special thank you

We all have people in our lives that have impacted us as human beings.

That English teacher who inspired you

The college professor left an imprint on your being

All pre-stroke, of course

NOW--- how to say thank you to those who made us laugh and cry sometimes; those who helped us jump start our journey.

There is and always will be a special love deep within our soul for each of them:

The doctors

The nurses

The therapists

The aides

Those that pushed us until we wanted to quit—they refused

to allow that

Whether pushing or pulling they made a difference

E can never say thank you in a strong enough word to

express our debt of gratitude

Some we will never see again

This is a painful reality

We can live content with the knowledge, they are off to parts

unknown to help others start their journey

God bless them everyone

These gifted souls these angels of mercy and grace

You are missed you and prayed for each day

The world is a better place with us in it (us stroke survivors)

The world is a better place with us in it

 This is true, if it were not so; we would all be victims and not survivors.

 As I've said before victims are not around to talk about their stroke; but survivors are.

 God spared us for a reason, our work here not yet done

 We must find our purpose and gifts and act upon them.

 I know my purpose in life is to help other people, especially stroke survivors on their Journey.

One of my gifts is writing and sharing my words with you is my blessing.

I try to live my life to make the world a better place sharing goodwill, joy and positive energy everywhere I go with everyone I meet.

Carpe Diem

Seize the day, Live today, it could be your last

We know how precious life is and how it can be shattered in

the blink of an eye.

No dwelling on our losses and who we were before. The past

is history

No regrets. Too late for that now

 No fretting about the future. The future is in God's hands

and we know the future

is a mystery

 Live in the present, (today) for that present is a gift from God

 Embrace and cherish time with family and friends

Today is all we have

Tomorrow is not a promise

Thoreau said it best, "Oh to reach the point of death...

Only to find you have not lived."

God gave us a second chance. Let us not be that person with regrets of not living life.

Live with gusto.

Self- preservation (A note to Caregivers from Us Survivors)

We don't know the struggles you face. We can't know them

It's not that we don't care. Of course we do! We just forget to ask.

We are obsessed with our basic humanistic instinct of SELF-PRESERVATION.

It will take some time eventually survivors will realize OTHERS are grappling with your own "New Normal".

Survivors ARE NOT selfish and self-absorbed (ALTHOUGH it is all about us, isn't it?) self-preservation is a step along the journey of the New Normal

Everyone knows the stroke affected the survivor Physically, Mentally and Emotionally.

Survivors need to understand the stroke's impact on the entire family.

Roles change, as do needs, For survivor, family and friends.

Together survivor and caregiver must determine their conjoined New Normal.

Things will improve, but it will take time; As survivor and caretaker begin their Journey of their New Normal. There are questions with no answers: why me? what now? what next?

The journey is long and everyone must acknowledge both survivor and caregivers need love and support. Of course the Survivor cannot see this; still struggling to break out of the wet paper bag we find ourselves in. We don't know your struggles We do care we simply forget to ask.

We are fighting: To get our old self back.   To stave off the depression. Fighting for self-preservation

Alas our struggles consume us, and what little energy we may have.

Roller Coaster

Life is a Roller Coaster; with its ups and downs of everyday
life. Somewhat predictable,

except for those unexpected life altering events, some are good some not so good.

roller coasters should be fun; many are.

reaching that Peak and knowing what lays ahead; the thrills, excitement and some fear.

 The mental emotional roller-coasters of stroke survival are unpredictable.

not thrilling nor exciting, However, many fears and questions without answers:

What? Why? Where?... How?...When?... Feelings of Personal guilt, frustrations

and a "shattered sense of self" .

 Quite often, we may be unaware of the magnitude and depth of our deficits.

 unable to see the Peaks approaching; let alone what lies ahead.

The paranoid thinking you are a burden to loved ones. Push those thoughts aside. they exist, only in YOUR mind.

Those loved ones stood or Sat by your side, during a challenging time for all.

 Making the medical decisions you could not. Their choices brought you to here and now.

When doubts arise; We need only recall, that budding love of oh so many years ago,

and the good times you shared. Of course life wasn't and isn't a bed of roses.

We must remember Adversity enters our lives not to destroy us; but to help us find our hidden potential.

We can take solace from the unconditional love bestowed upon us by:

 children, grandchildren, family and friends. Find serenity with those memories

Rejoice to be here enjoying life.

RISING

Like the phoenix rising from the ashes

As a Stroke survivor, I see myself rising from the ruins of a shattered/ broken man.

A mere shell of the man I was before 11-12-13

Destroyed physically mentally emotionally vocationally

Many Trials and errors attempting to pick up those pieces of my pre stroke life.

Multiple Attempts Fail; not for lack of effort or desire.

Even if the pieces can be found, they will not match up.

Like a bad jigsaw puzzle the pieces won't fit together

Much Like Humpty Dumpty no one can put the old me back together again

Reinventing, redefining or rediscovering ME!

Still a:

Husband, Father, Grandfather, Brother, Uncle, Friend to so many.

Now a poet once again.

My gift of writing Pushed aside all those years ago; life you know.

I am humbled and blessed to be allowed to share my words with the world.

So therapeutic to record my thoughts and feelings. Simply writing them down helps me sort things out and make sense of the new me in my New Normal.

MOSAIC

Like any shattered dish;

 The pieces of the shattered self must be picked up

Then sweep aside those shards that are too small to handle.

It will take time, but many pieces will be found

Another question arises, what to do with the collected pieces?

Sort and repurpose them, as a Mosaic.

The old you can never be again. However, when the pieces are arranged in the proper order

Whatever that is! The mosaic will be just as beautiful as the former you ever was.

The new you collecting pieces of your shattered past

 Creating a mosaic of you today.

For many of us, our words are our mosaic, whether blogging or writing poetry simply sharing our journey: The ups and downs, Good times and bad times too, The joys, stumbles, Falls and fears

Never giving up hope.

Those individual pieces, taken alone, represent a mere fraction of our previous life

The adhesive that holds those pieces in place Is the grace of God

After hard work and determination, A vision appears, created in the Mind's Eye of the artist

The mortar between all those pieces is: the love of family and friends

The finishing touch of the Mosaic is acceptance

Or better yet," hopecentance".

Acceptance of us here and now.

Yet, never giving up hope for the future.

New normal

Hey doc thanks for saving our lives! Now can you fix us?

We only want to be the person we were before the stroke.

We know you're not Houdini, yet we thought "no harm in asking".

There is no fix for us? What are the options?

Just the "New Normal." What is this New Normal?

The New Normal is what you make with what you have.

It has been sNew Normal it is not good nor bad but simply different.

Each of us has our own New Normal.

Unable to do all the things we did pre-stroke, those things that can be done are at a much slower pace.

Now we give hope to others, any way we can.

Shared stories inspire

Laughing at our deficits, without laughter there would be tears.

No way to connect the dots. Linear thinking and sequencing seem impossible.

A challenge to remember things for more than 30 seconds

Some cannot drive others travel by bus.

Some may use a walker, cane or even a wheelchair. At different times, many of us have used all three.

New normal Cont.

some have lost the ability to speak at least initially, with hard work and determination along with a good speech pathologist. The skill of speech may return, then some won't stop talking, making up for lost time?

At times, the words just won't come out. Frustration; knowing what the words are yet unable to make the sounds However, with frequent contacts with fellows Fighters we finish each other's sentences.

Some write to bring joy to self and others.

When walking more than a block, frequent rest breaks may be required.

At times still walking with limp requiring constant reminders to pick up the affected foot.

Visual impairment can lead to many apologies. Constantly bumping into people everywhere: shopping, the library, and the bus. Quite adept at apologies and brief explanations.

Most are understanding, yet others choose to just glare.

Buffet lines present unique challenges. Massive fears, bumping into people before you in line and spilling food on them and the floor. Frustration and Embarrassment are inadequate explanations of emotions in that moment.

Constant self-talk, "slow and steady wins the race".

. We acknowledge our blessings to be alive and still fighting. We learn to "live with" or even "accept" our new normal. Making the best with what we have.

Negativity

Negativity I have neither the time, space nor interest to have

you in my life

I know your strength

The power of your hooks buried deep within the souls of the

unsuspecting

I will not be sucked into your downward spiral

I was there, not too long ago

I kicked and clawed to escape your grip on me.

I proved to myself that I am stronger than you.

I refuse to return to your darkness

When you attempt to sneak back into my life

I push you aside

I choose to live my life in positivity.

No Pity PLEASE

Offer me not your pity

I had enough from myself throughout 2014, to last a few life

times

There is neither need nor desire for pity from me, you or

anyone

Join me and rejoice that I am alive!

If I stumble which happens now and then, please do not

jump in and start pulling me

Ask iirst, if I am okay

Then offer your assistance, if your help is needed I will

graciously accept

If you feel the need to brush off the dust and dirt, again

please ask if you can

I am thankful you are in my life.   No pity please, I am happy

and having fun. I share my words and story

If you feel the need to comfort me. Put your arm around my

shoulder, give me a hug, or just hold my hand a minute.

Reassuring me I am okay, and everything will be fine

I am grateful for your concern and being there to support me

I ask not for pity, please leave me my dignity

As good as it

What if ...

This is as good as it gets?

If this is as good as it gets, I am extremely

blessed and fortunate

I have my life. My family, My friends, Old

and New.

Standing by me as I need, as only they can. I

do the same for them.

I live my life as an example of

humanitarianism

I have rediscovered the poet deep within

me.

I share my words and story with many,

giving hope to many as they continue their

journey of The New Normal.

Inspiring others to return to their personal

journey writing poetry.

I am happy that my survival story helps so

many.

If this is as good as it gets

I'M OKAY WITH IT.

Rejoice

Prior to my stroke and my brush with death.

I appreciated life. I must admit, life is so much sweeter now

I now have time, and I take it, to watch the sunrise and listen to the birds sing as the day begins

Rejoice with me I am alive, I am happy and I am having fun

I try to make a difference every day.

I am meeting people, forging new friendships

Surviving my stroke brought me to here and now, Will you rejoice with me?

I am alive and I love it the life I'm living

All survivors are here by the grace of God, and many prayers, I am sure

The only question that remains,

What have you done today to express your gratitude?

For this second chance at life?

Small victories

All victories should be celebrated. Large or small, EVEN
THOSE unobserved by others

For those that have not survived a major life-altering event,
(especially any head trauma)   cannot appreciate the many
mini victories. Many can't appreciate our small victories, for
example:

Remembering someone's name

 Carrying a cup of coffee with the affected arm/ hand and not
spilling it

 Successfully navigating a buffet line, without bumping into
anyone

Surviving grocery shopping; remembering to take the

grocery list and remembering to look at it

Getting through the store without bumping into anyone or

knocking over any displays.

Noticing improvements in walking, after years of recovering

Finally feeling secure enough in your balance to take a

shower standing,

All victories must be embraced and celebrated. They give us

the strength and courage to persevere.

Happiness

Happiness is a personal emotion uniquely defined by each of

us. In happiness, you can find true wisdom.

Our Happiness is in our control and our attitude plays a major role. We all find happiness in our own way.   Some find happiness helping other people.

Finding inspiration from those inspired by our words and stories.

Still others find happiness deep within simply living, loving and embracing life.

 Happiness is: sharing written words, a warm blanket, a warm worn sweatshirt

A gentle touch of a hand, a hug, reassuring words from a friend, in a time of need

Happiness is the unconditional love of a child, and the laughter of children.

Happiness is sharing time with good friends who make you laugh and feel loved

Being treated like a human being other people care about.

While shopping, remembering to look at the grocery list, if you remembered to take it.

Realizing minor improvements, even years after a stroke.

Loving yourself for who you are now.

Redefined.... Reinvented....Rediscovered.

Pulling oneself out of the darkness into the light of day.

With help of course, THANK You

Surviving to see two new grandsons added to the clan.

Happiness is a warm smile and a hearty, how are you today?

Sharing survival stories with others and providing them hope and encouragement,

Others claiming your story gives them hope and inspiration.

Looking back realizing how far you have come on your

journey, always moving forward.

Having more good day's than bad days.

Recovery

Some say recovered. Others say recovering.

Are they synonymous? You be the judge. For some the term Recovered indicates an end. While recovering anticipates continued improvements.

Some improvements may be so small they are unnoticed by others.

 Only you see or feel those subtle improvements.

For People in recovery there is no need to compare yourself with others.

 Every individual has unique life experiences

For Stroke survivors; every stroke is different. Mild, Moderate, or Severe. Unsure how to quantify these

We had a stroke and "life as we knew it, no longer exists."

A task is to redefine, reinvent or even rediscover oneself.

Every recovery is unique. As is every rehabilitation

Some similar recoveries may include: Physical, mental, emotional, speech and social recoveries.

There are no set steps, no playbook, only hard work and determination on your journey of the New Normal.

Oasis

Everyone needs an oasis

Everyone has them

Some may be shared with others

A single person or group may be an oasis

An oasis, offers a safe place of refuge from a desolate environment or desperate times.

They are life sustaining providing a pleasant contrast to daily toils.

A place you are treated with dignity, respect and love.

A place to clear the mind and collect thoughts.

There are many types of oasis; support groups may be an oasis. For stroke survivors, the stroke support group is an oasis. It matters not if the support group is live, (face to face) or virtual (online), both offer invaluable support and comfort.

A place to ask question or discuss concerns, with others who truly understand

For some the support group oasis is a break for the caregivers, yet others may view it as a break from their caregiver

Can you identify your oasis?

OOPS, I'm sorry but I didn't see you.

The hidden disability creating more challenges

There is no way for you to know,

About my stroke and blindness, unless of course, I tell you.

I am blind, I feel so sorry! No, not for myself,

I'm sorry for anyone that has had an unfortunate encounter with me,

throughout my recovery. (Nov. 2013 to present)

I apologize to those I have bumped into, or hit with a grocery cart

Or those I may have inadvertently tried to sit on, while on the bus.

Most people are very understanding with a brief explanation and apology.

Others choose to just glare

bus buddies just push me aside and we laugh together.

A multitude of Emotions: Frustration initially; Which turned to Embarrassment,

 it took a while, but I finally realized

Frustration, embarrassment and sadness about my losses will change nothing

I turned to humor, laughing at my deficits and related incidents (no harm)

one day it turned to humiliation

Embarrassment was hard enough to work through

No need to humiliate me, by screaming at me. When I almost sat on someone on the bus.

I said I'm sorry. What more could I do to make things right?

The only thing left to say is, "Oops, I'm sorry, but I didn't see you.

APPENDIX

A FEW OTHER POEMS, I WANTED TO SHARE

We are human

We are human. That is a statement of explanation not an excuse

"HUMANS" They are here, there and everywhere

There goes a Jew, a Catholic, a Mormon, a Muslim, a Buddhist, a Christian

We are all different, yet all the same, we are all human.

Look at them there:

Long hair, Short hair, even in-between hair, no hair, Red or Black hair, even Green.

We are all different

Yet the same

We are human.

Body piercings everywhere, Ears, Noses, Lips, and tongues, others better left unknown.

There goes a Lesbian, Gay, Bi-sexual Transgendered Punk, Hippie, Rocker, Writer, Artists

Peel away the labels; what is left?

US Each special in our own way

Accept us or reject us

 No need for labels they only create barriers between us.

We are different

Yet everyone the same you see

For we are here to share this time and space

If only for a while.

We are human. We must:

Live together, Work together, Know each other, Trust each other, And Love Each Other

We are all humans why can't we just be?

Just Hangin' at the E. (Th Exquisite Corpse Coffee House)

(the Exquisite Corpse Coffee House

Hanging' at the E, a place where you can see,

the artist known as me.

Just hangin' at the E my artist buddies and me

Sharing a coffee, conversation, and collaboration

 If struggling for a word or phrase

Others help to fill that gap

We share joy, when the work is done.

A special place the E

A place where any artist can just be.

Sitting here with pen and coffee in hand

I write my word for thee.

There's Coffee in my table

Rocking in my chair,

in the open air,

watching the silent fanfare,

 Push away despair

Biding time... until I go... To Parts Unknown to me

I write my words, then file them

Just Hangin' at the E. Con't

to share another day,

I write so much while at the E

Sharing time and space with artists just like me.

All welcome at the E., Aspiring just to be...

Piano players, painters, clay throwers, Poets, novelists, mixed media, just to name a few.

 You name the discipline the artists have been here

Each Leaving behind. A trace their creative energy from deep within their artist's soul,

Left for others to embrace and do with as they please. Take only what you need

When the time is done, please leave behind, your own creative force. For, yet another to consume.

Each ensuring that we leave behind as much as we have used, to keep the balance of the ying and yang

A very Special Place to me.

Hanging at the "E"

Restless writer

Does the restless writer write because he can or because he must?

There is a need to write. Restless thoughts fly about, juggling multiple projects at once.

A simple word or phrase is all that is required, to release the creative flow.

A few words here, then a few words there; back to here to tweak it just once more.

Writing words as they enter the mind

later to determine where they best fit, which poem and location

These words tell a truth; or maybe just a story of inspiration or introspection.

When least expected, there it is a word or phrase that begs to be…

Embellished far beyond a word or two

Creativity is uncontrollable, one can only hope to focus it, one can never force it a writer must… be prepared when the thoughts begin to flow.

There are times keeping up with the words seem impossible

The restless writer carefully searches for that perfect word or sequence.

It seems time slips away when the words begin to flow.

Words are scarce tine seems unending

The urge to write grows strong. The words elude and evade. Like trying to stack marbles.

So so close then words slip away. The words that must be written tease and taunt the restless writer.

The restless writer writes because he can or is it because he must?

Mst... release the energy within, or fulfill the dream of sharing his given gift of wring.

These words all spoken several times before; certainly not in this chosen sequence.

These words belong to all of us; the restless writer is just an instrument.

Simply a means of recording these sequences of words; intended for the entire world to share.

The written word comforts the soul and soothes the mind.

beauty of life the gift is honored.

The restless writes because he can and because he must.

Friendship

Friendship is defined in many unique ways.

There are Old friends, new friends not yet met friends.

There are times when people meet and in that instant a connection is made.

No one can explain the how or why.

From that moment on the bond of friendship grows.

With each hello and goodbye and shared laugh.

Friendships take time to develop, with care and nurturing the bond will grow strong.

Strengthened with each how is your mother, brother, sister, husband, wife?

Relatives never met, but with the friendship and the connection made, the concerns are understood.

Thoughts and prayers are offered. (If the need is greater many would chose to be there)

Friendships grow stronger with frequent encounters.

Perhaps forged in shared adversity.

Similar life altering experiences and Shared words.

Never embarrassed to ask for nor accept assistance.

Supporting each other side by side; equals in every way.

Prepared to provide whatever is needed.

By your side during times of struggle or frustration.

With A fist Pump, Handshake, hug comforting words, or listening heart.

A shoulder to cry on or even stand upon to keep ones head above the swirling waters of daily life; rushing past like a tsunami.

The bonds of friendship much like the threads of a spider's web can be very strong yet fragile just the same.

True Friendship stands the test of time; Weeks, Months, even years may pass.

After time apart, an encounter with a friend results in warming of the heart and soul and smiles aplenty. Chatting like old times, as if no time has passed at all.

Friendships are dear to the heart. They are needed for human survival.

On Your Wedding Day

 On this your wedding day; as the sun rose this morning you awoke as two separate independent individuals.

The forces of nature brought you to each other and to this day.

Look around you; your family and friends are here to support you, not just today but long into the future, in any way they can

Now as the day comes to an end with a Setting Sun.

We say goodbye to this YOUR day and to those two separate individuals.

Tomorrow you will awake two as one.

And begin your new life together.

May your life together be filled with love, joy, Blessings and fun.

70955170R00046

Made in the USA
Middletown, DE
19 April 2018